When I Reach You

When I Reach You

poems

Dean Olson

2015 · FITHIAN PRESS
MCKINLEYVILLE, CALIFORNIA

Printed in the United States of America

Many of these poems were inspired by the 14th-century Persian Khwāja Shams-ud-Dīn Muhammad Hāfez-e Shīrāzī, known by his pen name, Hafiz.

"Cheap Seats" appeared previously in *The Georgia Review* and *Off the Clock*, Fithian Press. "Gentle Reader" appeared previously in *The Lyric*.

"Leaving," "The Laboring Oar," "On Being Elder," "Straightening," and "Fall Walk" appeared previously in *Crossing*, Fithian Press.

"Hotter than Body Heat" appeared previously in *Off the Clock*, Fithian Press.

Published by Fithian Press
A division of Daniel and Daniel, Publishers, Inc.
Post Office Box 2790
McKinleyville, CA 95519
www.danielpublishing.com

Distributed by SCB Distributors (800) 729-6423

LIBRARY OF CONGRESS CATALOGING-IN-PUBLICATION DATA
Olson, Dean, (date)
[Poems. Selections]
When I reach you : poems / by Dean Olson.
pages ; cm
ISBN 978-1-56474-788-4 (softcover : acid-free paper)
I. Title.
PS3615.L7337A6 2015
811'.6—dc23

2015002587

Contents

I.

II.

I.

Plumbing the Well of Love

Love is like a late spring.

Trust is slow coming
until hearts fully enfold
an upwelling of love,

we learn there is nothing to confess,
no shame, no blame
in plumbing the well of passion.

We make love across the page
and into the margin
for the sheer joy made

weighing no guilt or sin
in drinking our fill.

Wakening

To recall home
is to remember
the bend of fruited branches

the bellow of cows to morning milk
stubble pheasants singing
in morning mist

the tongued chill
of a palmed creek.

I would lie in this field again
with empty hands and aging heart

and under late summer skies
see miles into myself

waken the free man
cleansed of illusion

of what I take
and what I leave.

The Overflowing

In these seasons of steady downpour,
slathering sump and guttural gutters,

I dream in the delicate dialect

of limbs freshly leaved,
the flush of fledgling in morning sun

the first corona of crocus,
the nascent frill of narcissi,

and feeling your soft
sheltering skin,

turn from the dreary distances

placing my trust in the tangible touching
we have come to know,

the lush larynx of love.

Sunrise

Praise sunrise!

All around things return to life
as they were.

Again fresh, again vigorous

as the moon shutters

and you light our bodies
as new leaves
eager and free, tenacious.

We lie now this way,
then that,

sway exuberant, liberated,
fleeing the musty wardrobe of night.

Evening Dreams

This is the time of year
wispy fingers of fog
enter orchards and fields.

They caress nude branches
leaven layered beds of leaves

embrace slender legs of bordering berry
cling to angular limbs of young maple.

They rest in quiet clouds above
warm bodies of slow breathing ponds,

and if we wish

will carry us over fields of love
wetting nest and stubble as we go.

Valentine

Now I'm old enough
to know what an old man thinks
staring into the distance

I often awaken to find myself
hip-deep in a river of memory,
age weighing me down
like stone in my pocket.

Then I listen to the untroubled rhythm
of your breathing,
feel the warm hand
of your body next to mine

and remember there is more to love
than making love.

An Arrow Always Falls

so for this moment pretend
    our love will time suspend

as leavened our bodies rise
    and into our heart love flies.

Though spring's lush arrow is cast
    I fear love's flight will not last,

so treasure the time we're given
    release the love you keep hidden.

When Daylight Is Going

When daylight is going
I learn what it's like to dream
of someone.

When I leave you each evening
the cave of my heart
echoes with words of parting

and I carry you into night
empty of thought otherwise.

I lean on you
when daylight is going,
you sleep with me until morning.

If my dreams should wander,
you cast from a great distance
and gather me in.

The Tiller

Furnished in burnished yew
fitted in a shoe of riveted steel,
fashioned to hand-held roundness,
knuckle ended, sweat cured,

well balanced and worn smooth
she travels with him everywhere
guiding his subtle touch.

Foretelling wind and current in braille,
she's a grainy head turner,
a seasoned story teller telling tales
in elusive tongue, the closest thing
to seeing and not seeing.

When the sea speaks his fingers
seem to enter the turned yew,
calculation gives way to unburdened habit
as a oneness compels him
to trust his phantom limb.

Morning Love

I wake with the sun and in my leaving
pull the sheet from your shoulders.

Your body shines like a star at dawn,
your face and tossed hair appear
as a flower with new-born foliage.

Gazing at your motionless body
the more I see the more I burn to see
and I want to love you
as morning sun consumes the dew.

Slowly you rise to my touch
like a fish from a still pond
and I whisper my wish to pleasure you,
to bring you fullest joy,
to slacken any thirst.

And as a moving stream must flow to the sea
we wrap ourselves in the last notes of dawn.

The Wardrobe

Now love has drawn me in
I've become so absorbed in your life
I feel as if my body lies helpless
as a garment in your wardrobe.

Here there is foreclosure of sound.
Cradled like a secret, I breathe other breath,
my dreams take flight
buoyed by the touch of silk,
the scent of your body.

I hibernate, furtive, in silhouette, fearing
discovery, yet so great is my need to feel
the groundswell of your love
I overcome fear, and am unwavering.

Lightheaded, I pray the door will open
and in a flood of extravagant light
you will reach in and draw me out.

Falling in Love

This stretch of sea my vessel's prow
now dares to cut is no place for a little boat
nor for a captain who would spare himself.
— Dante Alighieri, Paradise, *Canto XXIII, lines 67–69*

Falling in love
is taking leave of surefootedness,
a letting go of familiar ground,
entering an unpredictable land
of shifting tenses.

Love is a narrow causeway
bridging uncertainty to a new place
where balance is steadied
with close touching,

one must trust there is an otherworld
which yields to lovers' weight
as if they are passengers
boarding a ferry letting on new life,
windblown and fresh.

Waking Alone

The morning sun rises soft and muted
as if it is your hand touching my thigh.
I wake with the warming while fluted
peonies rise greeting the sun's first light
and the owl rests from moonlit labor.
And though my bed now lies fallow
you bring to life a loving flavor
as memories of your hair on my pillow
leave lattice weaves in the lessening haze.

I rise slow as the opening rose
weighing the melancholy life plays
while on the ceiling gathering light sows.
With the waking over I see the day through
doing the things you would have me do.

Autumn Vows

Come into the night my dear, draw near now.
Let us sit beside the fresh-mown hay,
recite to one another our loving vows
intoned many years ago this very day.
Praising new love we hoped would last,
we sculpted our love this cherished night
embracing one another in a lovers' clasp,
as the fall moon spread its whispered light.

Come, let bodies brittle as aged willow
grow warm and supple as love flows,
while field owls mind the darkened furrow,
memory will youthful vigor bestow.
Come my dear, sit with me under the moon.
Renew the vows that made our love bloom.

Bipolar Love

after The Letters of Vincent van Gogh

When life weighs heavily upon me
and my steps falter, only with another
can I be saved.

Otherwise my life passes over
what once was a face
as in the mirror my face dissolves like water
and life leaks away.

When I am with you life returns.
Your love becomes sap pulsing in my limbs
and time resumes as the world we knew
comes back to me.

Soon I hear sparrow in the gutter,
jay in the holly and grow impatient
to join you in fields of spring flowers.
It is as if you have conquered time.

As Spring Tempers the Leaf

To lose sight and touch of you
as in winter, is to no longer be.

I find myself in a place
without time or light;
where darkness is endless,
cold rends my limbs
and life becomes unbearable.

I endure until you warm me
with heated breath
draw me again to lips
pouring light everywhere.

You compel me to renew.

I become exuberant
and there is little time
for other things.

All is given until once again
there is nothing to give.

What Appears So Is So

...as the heart grows older
It will come to such sights colder...
—Gerard Manley Hopkins, "Spring and Fall"

The leaf's gift of color fades
As fall wind spreads over its face
And slender stems yield and sigh
Torn from leaves that broken lie.

When the moon lights a scene dire
We draw nearer the dreaming fire.
Through falling snow our dreams go
Whispering, "What appears so is so."

Now springs upon springs blend
And wandering color has again fled.
A cold wind spreads over bodies old
Whispering, "Soon the old must go."

We gather our coverlet of love near
Answering "We have little to fear."

In a Dream

In a dream fleeing from everyone
I am drawn down and drawn down
until beneath me there is no ground.

A hand reaches from the jetty
like a thread
and you draw me in to play with,
to lie about with.

You take me by the hand,
show how love pleases,
how love swells to bursting
like a peach plucked fresh.

You become the tree
to which I cling,
my cries muffled
in the holy ground of our love
and I am submerged in sorrow
no more.

When He Brings Her

for Marge 1937–2002

Our grandson is her in every way.

It is as if their lights mingle,
and now she's gone
in him she is both hidden and manifest.

He mirrors her furrowed brow
as we play with cars on the floor
comparing design and color.

When he listens to music
while eating breakfast in his pajamas
she is the fountain of sun in his eyes.

As we watch the cat watch the birds
in the shade of a willow and talk about why,
she is his strength.

When he steers the old pickup from my lap
with deep throaty growls,
I smell her in his blonde hair.

And when his mother comes for him
I clothe my soul bird
in a quilt of silent songs.

When Everything Else Is Prologue

Watching the sun rise I see how night flees,
how it hauls itself into the shadows
and think how differently love
leaves a dense forest,
enters a broad estuary where shadows fade
and everything is made clear.

Love flows like a river
from the dark nest of my body
carrying selfishness, sadness, and doubt,
fear and disappointment to the sea
where they lose buoyancy and intention.

I enter a place where cravings are fulfilled,
I love openly without possessing,
without expecting,
simply holding my heart open.

The Whole of Spring

after Rainer Maria Rilke, Duino Elegies

For years he lives a thinly settled life.
It is not there are few around him,
he simply knows others as one knows
the shell of things, as things countable.

He prefers solitariness to the flesh of feelings,
tends life as an accountant his ledger,
absent the unfathomable mess of affection
sitting in silence behind his heart's curtain.

He lives in endless outcry, not at home
in or out his body of imageless stone
until love calls him from the hushed stillness
and ordinary life is no longer enough.

Now his entire body trembles as love seeps into him,
enters his blood unknowable and silent
like fruit swelling in a warm glen
or the lingering tongue of aged wine.

He is the whole of springtime
floating like dew on morning grass.

The Ball

For her the ball is a ritual dance
around which entreating hearts
weigh willing grace and wellness
as young bodies pass in review.

Perfumed scent trails in streams
as she glides with an indifferent light
playing in her eyes, passion corseted
tightly against her body as if a portrait,

until all at once she fans her gown into flame,
blood wells up and the serious work
of pressing tomorrow's bedding begins.

He imagines the distant call of night birds,
hips and thighs a flare,
virginity loosened like long hair.

Rue the Land

My friend wraps a childhood
of green plenty around her,
recalls orchards of ripe fruit,
fall meadows in bloom.

She remembers gestures of opening flowers,
lying with the scented sea on cool evenings
as with an old friend,
breathing the sea's patient cadence
as stars open their gift.

Then, at first harmless, inconspicuous,
wearing the unassuming cloche of a warm candle,
the sky, as if leaning on the lip of the sun's limb,
ceases to cool.

Stubborn neighbors, believing nature is never spent,
unable to lay aside their habits,
hide indifferent hearts in salesman satchels
as soils boil, change color.

And childhood places,
condensed by the weight of centuries,
reduce to sour rue.

Cougar

You who captures the heart
of a man who wanders
pathless in a dark forest,
take him into the warm valley
of your arms.

You who moves like moonlight,
knowing he belongs to no one,
cover him with soft heather,
weave your spell over him,
fill his heart with peace.

You who slumbers in morning,
swell in his hands like a grape
as he is absorbed
and utterly disappears.

Discovering Love

As if climbing from loose soil
to complete life in one brief season,
she longs desperately for a foothold,
her need ringing like a bell
renouncing any goal but love,
the imagined delight of concentrated reality,
of naked clarity.

She views love as the inducement to ripen,
the urgent work for which all other work
is preparation.

But when she bites the fruit of life,
when she places her hand on a man's shoulder
seeking her body's purest, deepest concentration,
she finds disappointment, an incompleteness,
the bitter taste of love simply taken.

Now she realizes love serves a deeper need,
the clarity she seeks through love
lies not as mere complement
but in unhurried shared discovery.

Unrepentant

Hearing her name called
she looks over her thin shoulder
to memories weighted
with the sweet aftertaste of love
sewn in the timeless pattern
of ancient weavers.

She has made an agreement
with what comes next,
has been taken into its confidence,
the numberless goings-on of life
softening to dreams of things to come;
wandering through deep valleys,
along crystalline lakes and sandy shores
in seasons bathed gentle and warm.

She wonders how it will feel
to swing in a sash suspended
by threads of her white hair
as limbs of aspen comb the air.

Worked Up Hard

Once when worked up hard
I craved your loving touch
To sooth my soul sore and scarred,
Was told I sought too much.

So I took my tormented body away
Bathed with salmon in slow streams
Swam with seals in shallow bays
Found within me a hidden spring.

Now I clutch my soul tight
At peace in solitude still,
And as morning light
Sounds the bell over the sill

Sail beyond the shallow bar
To once again journey far.

Dixieland Jazz

When I dance with my
close bosom friend
we celebrate
the swift swirling floor
of rosy hued faces and hems
of lace.
And sometimes, hand in hand
we whirl round conspiring
to trace
love's budding promise,
a summer's end we hope never
to face
when reed and string lie still
and resting hearts keep a
lover's pace
as hair soft lifted by
winnowing air lies
in place.

When I Reach You

My journey is made long
by the pure joy I hold inside
to stir me on still nights,
warm me on windy days.

I will be old when I reach you
with nothing to give
but tales to tell,
songs to sing.

I will be poor when I reach you
with nothing to give
but my cargo of love
fresh as flowers.

I will be worn when I reach you
with nothing to give
but a heart hewed
by your love.

In the Garden

She comes to sit in the garden
though now what is near seems far
and framed in dreamlike distance.

Flowers are still-life with no crisp edge,
as if caught in rain, or hidden beneath ripples
she cannot rub from her eyes.

As morning sun warms memory
she smiles and the garden comes to life
in the bright light of her youth;

the sweeping perfection of each petal,
the bold body of every leaf and stem,
the swelling tongue of iris.

At home her mind dances with images
until the scheme of things slowly goes out of her,
like a butterfly fluttering out to sea.

Stubble

Oh, how new stalks tease me
with untrammeled spirit, slender limb,
near weightless body, crimson hair
magenta hued in the heat of noon,
moist and lazy with evening dew.

How I long to stay and would
were I not last season's stubble, colorless,
shapeless, smelling of turned soil,
almost make believe, peeking warily
from here and there, wearily

gleaning memory as your life begins,
what is left of mine goes home again.

When Troubles Fall Away

I sit on my porch watching
a fledging chickadee peck at brown grass.
A family of house wrens scratch beneath the empty feeder.
A crow escapes the heat nearby, beak open,
wings spread in the shade of a maple.

As my body sleeps I dream
of breaking away from the sweltering coast.
Troubles fall away as I feel the cool offshore trades
tickle the whole of my body again,
the wife and kids left at home.

Things move slow in the heat.
In evening the crow leaves for the roost.
The chick returns to its tree house, the wren to an old stump.
I open the wine, slice apple and cheese,
wash the taste of guilt from me.

Drawing Near

The thought of drawing near you
opens me to contentment,
peels away the face of importance
I wear in the company of others.

Drawing near you cleanses me
as soft rain on a summer day,
your fragrance compels me
as a bee drawn to moist nectar.

Divining the fruit of harmony,
seduced by your siren call
I am driven to touch you,
take your breath in mine.

A Solace of Apple

I knew before entering the house.
Walking down the driveway, I knew.
Mom had baked apple pie.

Aroma filled the air like melody
floated around me and through me,
carried me along.

Everything else about the day is fragment;
who was there, what we talked about,
other bits and pieces,

but to the apple pie, the way it filled the air
with the rhythm of all that was good,
I still give myself. This is mine.

Remembrance

She took her mother's worn shirt
to keep near the smell of her body.
She took the answering machine
to keep near the sound of her voice.
She took the quilt her hands had stitched
to keep near the soul of her work.
She took pictures from the wall of her room
to keep near what her mother would see.
The more she stood beside her, slept
beneath her, journeyed with her,
the more she knew and loved her
and longed to join her in the ocean of space.

A Depleted Life

I knew life was leaving him
when cigarettes burned his fingers
as he watched the tide pull back.

At first I imagined him deep in the past,
the silky bottom pulling him
as the ebb exposed forgotten shapes
from an invisible world.
Perhaps he is a single man strutting
around town like a pheasant in corn stubble,
perhaps a worried father listening
to the quiet of a morning wood
before the sound of his saw takes it,
thinking how fate fastens him
to yet another stand of trees.

Soon we would lose him.
His life was used up
and like a stuttering candle loses touch with flame,
his mind was losing touch with his body.
I was not ready for this, not ready at all.

Night Harvest

after viewing a Night Harvest Cabernet wine label

She reaches out as if caressing
the crescent moon to fill
lighting the night harvest,

stretches her body over the thick stalk,
combs aside the covering canopy
moistened by evening dew,

ladders eagerly into the lush stirrings,
the plump fruit she claims.
She tongues the concentrated flavors,

fingers the ripe fullness covetously
as it rests within her palm
fervent and willing, and then

swiftly guides the startled cluster
into her harvest basket
to foment and flower.

Pied Beauty

after Gerard Manley Hopkins

At first I was attracted to you
as night moth to flame,
the indifferent union of dark and light
compelling me to draw near.

Embracing, you awakened me,
opening my eyes to all things possible
in night or day, in coupled gray;
the dappled finch's wing,
the stippled trout, the freckled breast.

Now I see the whole in every part
what can I do but love you?

On the Road to Damascus

after Second Space, New Poems, *by Czeslaw Milosz (2004)*

It begins immediately, behind the smooth face of youth.
Time is busy applying wrinkles.
Shame and regret trouble the untroubled mind
erasing smiles from our lips.

As if in accordance with arcane doctrine
ash is sprinkled in our hair,
ears grow silent,
and the prick of a tiny thorn releases torrents.

Sunday school notions of immortality are sacrificed
in the flaccid humiliation of bedroom mirrors,
and because it is said we are created in His image,
we wonder which deity we resemble.

Being so changed in life we wonder what will happen in death,
to those who haven't fully lived,
those who embraced enlightenment,
those who invoked the adequacy of human tongue.

A Place for Ritual

Someone said to be human is to be
a transitional species experimenting
with an enlarged brain,
an alien amid the galaxies.

Perhaps this is why, maimed by self-doubt,
we were drawn to ritual
as penance of the unintended,
to explain the human condition, give it texture.

And why, even though
we had never wronged the galaxies,
had nothing particular to confess

we felt tended, and if not the center,
at least a part, of something grand,
kneeling before high altars of resignation.

Until some among us opened books
in newly wired cottages
and the Angel of Passivity outlived its term.

When Thought Is Life

Thought is life, want of thought is death.
—William Blake

Religious doctrine argues
thought is a tariff
levied on humankind,

that quality of life suffers
if we shy from help
carrying the burden.

We come to believe it is safe
when thought flows in channels,
collects in whirls contoured by others.

We go about, our burden lightened,
indifferent to carving meaning
we might sculpt ourselves

contrary thoughts are swept aside
like seed pods
flowing unopened out to sea.

Autumn Uncertainty

Deer move slowly through brown fields,
under barren orchard trees, past rows
of yellow raspberry, lifeless leaves
of withered squash. Creatures of habit,
the deer follow summer paths of plenty
some will travel again in spring.

We watch the slick russet fold
of winter coats move with each step,
how some hold their heads with a certain
air of confidence, while others bend noses
near the ground.

We wonder who we will see again
when chipmunks gossip, blackbirds sing
and alder leaves whisper
to a chorus of tree frogs,

who we will find while gathering holly,
hold as emptiness until winter ends.

Knob and Tube

In the beginning,
the wolves of Aesop and Grimm
grinned a lantern-glow yellow,

the path to the well narrowed as night
swallowed the sliver of day beyond the hill,
all manner of things imaginable climbing
from the hollow well,

fire flicker from cook stove vents
flashed faces on the galvanized wash tub
as mother's water scoop poised overhead
like a raven's beak,

the moonlit flimflam of aspen leaves
clawed my cold attic window
like frozen hands of homeless children,

until knob and tube wiring
opened the page fully, drove night
from the kitchen, mystery from dancing shadows,
washing everything in deliberate pastel.

Keats

after Posthumous Keats, *by Stanley Plumly*

Even when a black sky
reigned over him,

even when a towering sea seemed
to fill his lungs,

as he searched for wind walking
the slightest hill
and his head whirled about him,

he could suck melancholy from life
as a weasel sucks yolk from an egg.

He set out to gather scraps and parts of life,
the grand seasons, wide meadows,
silent cathedrals,

hastened to pen verse before his name
was written in water
and he traveled to green and golden realms,
wild and free ranging.

The Center

as many men who think themselves
the center....this many are fools

You are my well, my inspiration.

When near you
I hear everything there is to hear,
see all there is to see,

my body feels the sharp tongue of the sea,
feels the quiet peace of a shaded forest,
the brisk wind of high desert,
the vitality of all things possible.

When you are away
I am a seed waiting the sun
and when you return,
all that tastes bitter is again sweet,
all that grows old is again young.

In our meadow of love
you are the center of life,
a garden where it is always spring.

With Love

Before love we lived in a neighborhood
of small pleasures, deepest feelings,
un-mined ore in the midst of a soiled crowd,
unable to sing in a garden of roses.

Chains of shyness held us from fulfilling
want or need and as we grew older
it was easier to want less, leave need
hanging in a musty wardrobe.

With love our lives are burnished treasure.
Shyness abandoned,
we stand naked and without shame
in the mellow loom of a lantern,
in the bright day of a meadow,
raised from the dark into a freshness
where we appear to one another as we are,
validated and vigorous.

Without Love

Apart from you I am a vessel with no way on,
indifferent to surroundings,
unable to weave meaning into life
though art or destination,
unable to feel beneath me
the pulsing rhythm of a moonlit sea,
feel through the soles of my feet
warmth in chilled meadows wet with morning dew.

All such things are mere distraction
until you draw near
and the window to my heart is thrown open.

You bring to life subtle changes
in a night sea, the resident sun imprisoned
in morning meadows. It is as if I feel
the rich texture of all things small and large
for the first time.

When Time Is Enslaved

Time loses all meaning
when lovers find one another.

Time's tyranny weakens
like heat from a winter sun,
its influence displaced
by possibilities kindled
when a rich vein of love
is discovered, probed tentatively,
examined with suspended elation.

The world is breathless,
held at bay
while enchantment is explored.
Tenderness reigns
as love arrives, unpacks its luggage
and prepares to govern.

Time is enslaved as lovers
lie in the warmth of their private sun,
creating new lives from recipes
handed down before time.

The Path to Love

It seems to me the path to love
is wanting to love more than be loved,
wanting to care more than receive care.

Witness those who bring attention to themselves
leading predators from children, the soldier
who covers a grenade with her body.

Such selflessness is clear to everyone,
becomes habit everywhere love seeds
tilled ground no longer shackled to selfishness.

And we are emancipated by our love,
as if we become a part of everything, and in certainty,
a part of things larger than ourselves.

Love Is a Loose-Fitting Gown

Love is a loose-fitting gown
that coaxes me to explore,
entices me to examine
reach out and touch
contours jostling in vague outline.

I imagine gifts veiled in shifting silk,
long to caress the body of love
whose scent I know
and would give my life to dwell
within the gown's confined light.

I am eager.
No, I am compelled
like a moth at twilight,
to lift the hem and fly inside.

When Your Hair Turns Gray

When your hair turns gray
and your body loses tone,
don't despair what you've become,
don't worry about the candle going out.

Something luminous inside
is waiting for the door to open,
a new you to venture out
and lie in the sun.

You will know carefree love
and an energy for loving
only graying people can know,

a refuge where you
and your companion make the rules
and time asks little.

What a wonderful thing:
to learn the truth on the last part
of your journey.

All I Know Is Love

All I know is love,
here and now,
for in this place
you make the world bearable.

Here, my spirit is lifted
by something natural in the air
that heals as the sea throws itself ashore,

humbled by something exquisitely primal
as salt and spray coat my face,

awakened by something distractingly delightful
as rain washes me with completeness
a waterfall would envy,

and now, as you warm my chilled body
with the heat of intimacy,
all I know is love.

Come Nest with Me

Come nest with me
when you no longer sleep
and have been turned out.

I will rinse your tired body
in the even dew of my meadow,
lay you down withered and shallow
on my bed of downy duff,
fluff plumy flowers for your pillow.

I will cover you tenderly
with lichen, moss and fern,
summon a winged chorus
to chant of love in cedar and fir.

The Quickening

About four months into pregnancy
certainty arrives as movement,
a posturing which quickens
to unrelenting brag,
the beginning of life's narrative
testing boundaries
with feet and fist.

Relishing its wetland sanctuary,
looking for an exit,
life searches for parallels,
curiosity becomes habit
and all movement
a sign of thirst.

Waiting over
the road sinks away,
calluses thicken with living,
the fever of movement falls
as thirst eases leaving
our stories in the woods
of autumn.

The Well and the Nib

I like to imagine you are my well
and I your nib bow to you
in the quintessence of love.

I lower myself into the indigo of devotion,
the melancholy of pacific blue,
meditative violet, elegant black.

My body craves your gift.
The spectrum matters little
as my nib wicks the luminous reservoir,
you hold the reins and I the addict
enter a sublime state,
and thereafter, for a time,
live an illusion of freedom,
until summoned
to the well once more by unrequited thirst.

But while my cheeks are in bloom
and my heart races, what songs I sing,
what tales I tell.

As Doors of Darkness Open

Night is a murmur,
a soothing plainsong deep in the bay.

Morning is the jagged hand of a clock,
a screech of heron, crank of hungry gull,
the raven's muscular summons.

The house steams in morning sun,
seeds stir the earth.

We uncoil, move stiffly
from the warm arms of bed,
enter the day's internment
as sunlight brushes the bay
with the smell of coffee.

We meet morning
like two colors fresh painted meet,
flare, and run together.

Remembering Our Bodies

after Twenty Poems of Georg Trakl

Silence and autumn snow
flow across the bay,
icy wind fingers our window.

Cold moonlight coats
our bodies blue,
leaves us in the uncertain light
of frail candle flicker.

We persuade ourselves
we are warm
and *are* warmed lying close
to memories of summer naps
in green meadows
and sun-warm dunes.

We own our affection,
leave nothing untouched.

In time our aging bodies
glow like ripe plums.

A Silent Interval

The bay is silent and still
the moment of high tide.

The sea comes inland
to take our measure,
looks us over,
then,
as if forgetting something,
leaves with a disinterested shrug.

The visit is a flicker,
a cosmic scribble
in the sea's melancholy tapestry,
a hovering examination
that goes unnoticed

as we milk the silent interval
for the out-of-sight dreams we find
in the quiet of our bed.

Sleeping Near You

At night when your sleeping body
heats me
as would a sun-warm stone,
I swell
like a grape in late summer.

Though we have lain together for years
my heart beats
like a fledgling's breast in first flight,
my skin blazes
hues of late autumn fields.

When the lamp of day lingers in your body
I dwell there
for I am tethered to you as a candle
to its glow.

II.

Leaving

He leans against the top rail,
elbows lodged tight as tent poles,
hands pressed to his cheeks,
toe-down boots heeled to the bottom bar,
shoulders cold-hunched,
back arched over the gate

waiting the first burst of spring,
that slender slice of morning magenta
slow-blending to thickened red and yellow,
molten, drawing the upper limb of promise
from beneath blue soil.

Behind him winter's long-nursed rage
whips field stalk and nude alder
with lingering savagery
as the sodden earth waits
to firm up, settle in and green.

He lingers hove-to
as a thin-rooted plant leans from wind
dreaming young dreams
beyond paying out hand over hand,
season after season,

until he is old enough to see
how life could be otherwise,
strong enough to follow the pull
as spring lifts the latch.

My Woman's Skin

In the vale of sleep
my woman's skin is silvery cool.

Touched, she rouses like the sun
opens flowers in spring.

I welcome nature's spectacle
beneath the coverlet of love,

yet at times long for islands of solitude;
to lie in my bed of thoughts,
open shutters to the cinema of memory
view distillations of life and illusion.

More often I cannot resist touching
the fragrant oasis of her life

purely to watch the morning flower open,
praise the prodigy of spring.

The Laboring Oar

I had no idea
the heaviness
of the laboring oar
she shouldered

until she laid it down,
left me alone
out of my element
feeling the heft of it

pull against the thole
as the loom fell,
the blade found
its task

and facing
into the work of it,
my back to the wind,
I understood.

On Being Elder

At last we touched upon the lonely shore
that never yet has seen its waters sailed
by one who then returned to tell the tale.
—Dante Alighieri, Purgatory *Canto I, lines 130–132*

I left any sense of creeping privilege at work
when I retired, or lost it elsewhere.
I longed for a community where elders
were sought out, made the center of things,
listened to. I envisioned telling stories to children
gathered at my feet. Tapping the reservoir of wisdom
ambassadors from the past are thought to possess,
I would draw lessons from folktales to mark
important life passages, carve moral boundaries.
But everywhere I looked the young
were like surfers mounting the crest of each moment,
riding the rush and lift of satellite and network.
Few had time to feel the slow steady pull of life,
enjoy the ordinariness of it, the pleasing work in it.
I came to see eldership as a nowhere,
an island no one willfully puts in, a strand
above high water where elders lie beached.
As I drew closer, I felt the sun's warmth,
noticed how it is elders glow as with the all-over
tan of the unclad, lament nothing,
lay aside the burden of emotional weight
to tend one another with a caring that asks
nothing in return, needing nothing more.

Fall Walk

A light September breeze carried
my father's sweat and wood pitch smell
away from the doe carefully picking
her way through salal and red huckleberry

so close we could hear the brush as she passed through
looking up from the shadows now and then
to chew and spoon sound into large ears.

These were the smells he brought home each night
to thicken like soup in the kitchen heat,
stirred now and then by the even hand of his voice.

The doe stood quietly trying to make
sense of things when the wind changed,
and one evening took him with her in last light

to return in fall as I walk with the heavy musk
of maple leaves, the acrid bite of fir pitch,
listening to the passing-through sound of salal and huckleberry
as it moves slowly aside and swiftly back.

Straightening

I want to witness the sea coming ashore
the whole of my life,
breathe her fresh whipped fragrance
lush with possibility.

I want to stand motionless before her,
walk slowly along the curve of her body,
bathe in the rainbow-hued mist,
listen to the compelling rhythm of her voice

as she rinses me of masquerade,
removes my masks of pretence,
straightens in me what the world has bent.

Gentle Reader

after Josephine Jacobsen

I will tell you how it is
when the trillium flower
and shafts of spring sun
light the leafing bower.

How the boy and I skirt
crocus bed and fiddlehead,
how he bends low
to clear webbed boughs
jeweled in morning dew,
whispers in my ear
as if we trespass
where voices startle deer.

How memory of his knees
against my cheeks
peels me like an orange,
juices me like a press
and I take it in pulp and pith
each time we go
to learn how the beaver dam fares,
if the big trout still lives there.

Hotter than Body Heat

Hotter than body heat in summer,
she made me quail and shudder
with visions of the possible
parceled neat to unseat the heart.

Lightsome and trim, tastily finished,
springy and straight, well shaped
hips with such swivel I imagined
music sweet as ringing bells.

I craned my head, held my breath,
balanced on planted balls and thus
at once rooted and buoyed my eyes glazed
as the garden of delight passed from view.

In the interval before time started again
I imagined my name called, a gate
thrown open and I the one chosen
to touch the moist garden of summer.

November

I've noticed my tree is without leaves. It happened all at once.
Only yesterday my neighbors were leaves and birds, now
everyone else has given in to winter's touch. I have
grown lonely, me and the bony sun clinging
to this barren waste out of habit and fear
falling so far. Soon I'll go to them,
the beds of faded leaves, thick
grass bent white from frost,
friends and family near.
I think it will be
fine being…
here.

Cheap Seats

We had to listen in our heads
as if watching a newsreel with lights dimmed,
the outline of it entering us.

Hearing the muffled voices
was like looking into the depths from a boat,
the sinew of thought, the intonations
a flowing river we could feel, intuit.

We crowded around voices mixed
with radio static and scratch,
making up the left out, the half imagined,
filling in what we wanted,
making the news accurate, the truth burnished
on the hard stone of experience.

We never lamented the silent spaces,
always emerged from them seeing things clearly
as if an old rightness had been confirmed,
drawn from the sound of rain,
the smell of fresh-cut wood.

My Father

My father was a common man,
a miner, logger, father of four sons,
a daughter.

There was a calmness, a solitude about him.
He spoke little, yet saw
all things that needed seeing,
and though he never spoke of love
I felt selected standing next to him,
so well made my bed of certainty.

My father was a short bald man
with heavy shoulders and strong hands.
He rose early and sometimes took his sons
to split winter wood or hunt winter food.
We watched and wanted to walk near him
as he ripened with age.

Though he has been set free
I sit beside my father now as if in the shade
of a giant willow. We touch for the first time
as the other world comes into mine.
He teaches the silence of simply doing,
the delicious taste of patience.